salmonpoetry

*Publishing Irish
& International
Poetry Since 1981*

After Love

Dani Gill

Published in 2017 by
Salmon Poetry
Cliffs of Moher, County Clare, Ireland
Website: www.salmonpoetry.com
Email: info@salmonpoetry.com

ISBN 978-1-910669-80-8

COVER IMAGE: *Self-Love* by FinbarMcHugh: www.finbar247.com
COVER DESIGN : Maureen Keith
TYPESETTING : *Siobhán Hutson*

Printed in Ireland by Sprint Print

*Salmon Poetry gratefully acknowledges the support of
The Arts Council / An Chomhairle Ealaoín*

Contents

Every person is like a piece of gold. If you were a gold ring, a gold watch, a gold chain, you could say "I am a ring, a watch, a chain", but these are temporary shapes. In truth, you are just gold – that is your essence, no matter how the shape changes.

Vedic metaphor

Ring

After Love

When the conversations are over
in your car, by the sea,
You are still here
and so am I,
after love.

I find myself in a small town
like the one I grew up in,
it sucks me in and down
I find solace at wooden tables in old pubs
with good friends and bad wine.
There is a lot to think about after love.

I dreamt last night about our parents,
mine talking about God
and trying to move furniture,
your father, a carpenter,
carving a long avenue
ahead of me.

I dreamt I went to meet you
in a house on a hill;
my underwear scattered everywhere,
your mother in the spare room
ironing, and when you appeared
you were much younger,
the shape of when we first met.
There was light in abundance

but I am no angel
and you arc not my god.
There is a lot to think about
after love.

Rings

A sapphire, diamonds, oval;
The rings our mothers thought I should have.
Standing at the window of Lazlo's,
wondering about a date, the year.

Driving down motorways
we made romance-less plans.
Talked about savings.
I felt myself fixated on tail lights –
each traffic jam, cause to imagine
ceremonies.

The plastic sandwich bag of models
has been packed away,
no demo was ever ordered
our mothers are shocked into silence.

I see them both in my dreams
drinking white wine and looking out windows.
I think they are still waiting
for an answer.

Rainy Evening

I pointed the car in the direction of home,
without thinking.
I was already at the granite counter
making tea and chatting with you.

It was hard then to drive
past the house where we first
made love
thinking of you
in your leather jacket
rain soaking the hide
laughing with me
at the door.
I brought you in
gave you a towel
looked into your blue eyes.

Tonight for the first time
I cry the kind of crying you hear
come out of yourself.
I am crying for both of us into a
blue towel, hair wet
from a lukewarm bath.

I dream you buy me a ring.
I am already wearing it as I search for a friend
in Woodquay.
There are people going for therapy
and my mother is telling me
how much you saved
how much you spent on me.

It was for me, wasn't for me,
the ring,
not quite right.
I could wear it, then exchange it
for something better down the line.

Someone Forgot to Mow the Grass

There by the shop. You had walked past it.
I was late to meet you.
I brought you to my house on top of the hill.
I made curry, but it was too spicy and
you didn't like mango.
I thought you were flirting with my housemate
and felt wounded.
That was the first time you came to my house.

The first time I came to your house
I shuffled behind you, nervous,
the outline of your mother.
I said I was OK but I was uncertain
there was so much to fit into.

Today, returning to your house,
the lawn is tall and full of summer
someone has forgotten to mow the grass.
There are flip flops next to the stairs,
the photos of me are all missing.

I climb steps and must go through our old room
through the bathroom where you've knocked
things over this morning – my things.
I pick them up and restore them.

Going through clothes, I carry as many as possible,
search through piles deciding what I cannot leave behind
cup books to my chest and I swear they have a heartbeat.

Finally, I find what I came for
in the second drawer.
The curtains are drawn and you are sleeping
on my side of the bed.

This book I am reading says guilt is destructive
it says we are allowed 'intelligent regret'.
I can take back my things
but I can't retrieve everything.
When these rooms are empty
my presence and my absence
will still be here.

The Crisis You Don't Know You're Having

Your heart beats faster
between gin evenings
and the morning after
images emerge, then dissolve.

You sing in the shower; you
look at the sea with what you think
is vacancy.

It nibbles away at nerve endings
heat spreads across your chest
you sleep nearer the edge of the bed.

The crisis you don't know you're having
finds you.

Single

Without you, that is my definition.

Today I thought of the ottoman
in your parents' living room
of sinking into cushions, soft tweed under my feet.

Today I thought of the ottoman
and of your father saying
One day the grandkids will lie on that.

Weightless

I bought a wetsuit
I went to the water
hoping it might tell me why
I felt so heavy.

I would just float
drift on my back
brain buzzing
silent fish circling
beneath.

The clouds look cloudier
when you're on your back
and the city lights further away.

Hugging my knees
alone at Blackrock
the season has changed
and I am still learning.

Today it is grief that I must dispel
and the grey waves carry me
they keep me up
I dive through them
across them
push myself
forward.

In the Year of the Sheep Goat

In the year of the Sheep Goat
a friend loses a child
then gives me a red rose.

In the year of the Sheep Goat
I meet a metal sheep and she
is not kind.

In the year of the Sheep Goat
conflicts do not cease
they evade, and cloak their activities.

In the year of the Sheep Goat
we crash through waves, find sand,
paddle in.

In the year of the Sheep Goat
situations become clear and then
everything darkens.

In the year of the Sheep Goat
one friend leaves and another
returns for good.

In the year of the Sheep Goat
the Horse is subdued and
the Monkey awaits its turn.

In the year of the Sheep Goat
there is loss and distrust
and then continuance.

In the year of the Sheep Goat
there are ideas, evolutions
and breakthroughs.

In the year of the Sheep Goat
some feel less afraid and others
grow insecure.

In the year of the Sheep Goat
there are crystals and candles
and new deities.

In the year of the Sheep Goat
skin is broken, muscle repairs,
fascia stretches.

In the year of the Sheep Goat
we tire of reading signs
we stop clocks and throw out calendars
turn inward for our answers.

Stamped

The untraceable mark
sheets and linens too heavy

2a.m. waking, fingers to sternum
searching for

the thing I will find so I
can understand how the weight of you
presses into me still.

Gold

Letting Go

In the shower I cup water in my hands
watch them
fill and empty, fill and empty.

Last week on your birthday
I sat on the edge of this bath and cried.
It seemed as good a place as any
for memories of our decade flooding.

My heart felt wrung-out after
an emptiness in my chest.

This morning in the shower
I cup water in my hands
watch them
fill and empty, fill and empty

I caught you and I let you go
I caught you and I let you go.

Key Line

I counted the hours until you left,
returned empty, to this car park
at the back of our house.

Sitting in my small green car
I watched the sun creep over the roof
of the cathedral-that perfect key line of dawn.

Fifteen minutes it took
until I could go in there.
Into our tiny flat.

My gut churned the answers but
I clenched them, I fought them
and ground them down
they were the dust that stuck
to your shoes in the evening.

I tried to be happy and I failed at it.
I broke both our hearts
but the crawling out of the grave feeling
that's gone now
in its place, a purer grief.

The Absence of You

Your nightmares aren't real but I am.

Close to dreams I think of you
and your absence.
How I *did* leave you.

How I will wake up tomorrow alone
and that this will happen
again and again
until sleep seems real and you
not real?

I turn out the lamp.
Continue.

Blackrock

Fleeing the clatter of pots
soft jazz, and conversation,
the ghost of you chases me
to the car, to the beach,
to the rocks.

Sunday was our day
and although another now makes me dinner
and my brother, high on gravy fumes, bubbles
through, grateful, I am haunted by
the memories of our Sunday afternoons,
the practiced rituals, nearly ten years old.

I drive and abandon the wheel,
walk barefoot in my suit to the water's edge
and sitting, knees to chest, I think
I am here, I am here, I am here,
to feel whatever the feeling is today,
and often it's a muddle these days,
the surge of a wave,
stones turning over.

Grief, like a cold pain shoots through my wrists,
into my shins, down the bumps of my ankles
and into this black rock.

It is rainy and I am grateful for it,
the spitting wind, the tide too high and full
for others – so just me, and this grey.

There are no answers in the sky or in the hills.
I breathe in, ribs rising under rubber skin,
push my hands into the stone
until they whiten,
curl toes and bend them to the sky,

and when I enter the black grey waves,
bobbing and bouncing,
this emptiness inside me is the buoyancy,
it keeps me up.

Osmosis

With the sea
still in my hair
I watch green lights
out on the water.

They've been here
each year I've lived
on this hill
looking over.

Today I know
someone threw down
the anchor, and I became rooted –
learned to be still.

Today in my bones
I feel an osmosis
from marrow to sinew
filling up and up
rising until
at the surface
it 'pops'.

Surfacing

I dive dive dive
down
chest pressed in

t-shirt wet against me
pull my body
down down down
to stone and pebble
collect one
pure white smooth

then up up up
through the blue
arms like levers
pulling pulling pulling

eventually I surface
wind on my cheekbones
salted, brined, returned.

Season

My clothes have changed
I wear new boots
and you won't see them

there will be no hanger holding
or dropped bags
in our hallway

I put on the new clothes
go into the world
embrace the season.

When a Shop Changes Its Name

It is still the same shop.
They scrape paint
and empty out onto the street
the cases and pots,
the metal things.

When a place becomes another
it harbours the former's ghost.
For months you will see familiarity:
lamps, chairs, cushions.

When something changes its name
it always remains the same.

Yin Yang

A stag and a fox meet in a clearing
surrounded by black trees.
Aerial view, a horseshoe,
the lines, yin in yang.

On a blanket of snow
the stag paces, waits for the fox
to come forward.

It doesn't, it hunkers low,
belly to the cold, watches the mist
of hot breath rising,
anchors to its position.

The Saturn Return

The judgement planet –
twenty-eight years in orbit –
has returned to teach its lessons.

Buckle up, knuckle down
you may become a master.
Consider country swapping
retreating or resist and dig deeper
to find your root.

When Saturn restriction
falls in, caution is exercised.
Pay attention to your ageing.
Lying low might be the way to go
while all of this happens.

Saturn is in my house now
I am ready to do battle.

Corpus Callosum

She says it happens to all women –
something clicks.
We change our diets or our partners,
doctor the career path.

She says it is natural.
My brain, you see, just needed
to fuse together, and in that moment
there was a switching;
something like clarity.

Chain

Snack Wrappers

With cold fingers we take them from their foil
our faces wind sunned and reddened
tea in an old school place.

If we've uncovered something
we've uncovered nothing
after seaside conversation
your eyes green as the water.

Cycling home, I feel a sadness
the crumpling of something
edges unwrapped and sharpened senses
a knowing of change.

These shape-shifting figures
who enter my life
leaving me with their wrappers
three of them in my backpack
when I get home.

Wintering

We wintered well
collars up, the newness
of things still crisp between us.

I had promised you a good winter
the warmth of me, your heart
tucked in my pocket.

We wintered well
kept each other out of darkness
you had promised me a good winter
my heart tucked in your pocket.

I don't remember cold
or short evenings
the light had no measure

I remember you, your hand tucked in my pocket
and going home under streetlamps
amber lit.

Piran

We took a trip to the pirate town
you could tumble into the sea there
a maze of streets like Venice
all corners and steps.

We bought prints in a gallery
rolled in brown paper
we took them up to the viewing point
a closed church
blue sea for miles and miles.

The frame maker gave them back to me today
two years late.
He says he remembers us coming in together
we intended them for our hallway
terracotta rooftops, blue sky.

I carry them in their bubble wrap
unsure what to do with them
wait until I am brave enough to look
and when I do, I see Tartini square,
Café Kavarna where we sat outside
watching that man in his seventies
skating and pirouetting around
half a dozen kids following him.

I remember it was a good day.

Nice, France (June 2016)

Isn't this the street?
Where our two-bed was to be?
Patio facing the sea
a doorway to the new town.

Weaving through crowds
I imagine your steps
twelve months ago,
with sunshine, without me.

The book I've bought
is a doomed love affair
wrapped in plastic, I take it
back with me.

Presentation Road

Always dark, always evening,
the heron stalking.
I named him 'Hiroshi' for novelty.
I remember calling you one night
asking if you'd walk toward me
the street seemed long and shadowy.

And your walk, the jaunt of it
coming to rescue me,
took me past number 15,
remember our jealousy?
That lovely Georgian door,
the hallway, the shuttering.
Our dream of one day maybe
owning that square meterage in
the city.

Past 12, where my parents
first lived, their lives cluttered
with a newborn, their intentions
to move up and out one day.

The empty site on the right,
where you could maybe build something.
Or 13, bay windows, glass backing
onto the river.

The stained glass of St. Joseph's
the black grey slabs before
the river, the small bridge.

Then 21, you and me,
one tiny floor for two people
starting off, settling in,
dreaming, wishing for each other,
making a life.

Matisse

(for Finbar)

Here, Matisse used pink, green, blue,
dabbed them in neat, single, squares
an experiment with colour.

I remember how you gave me a paint can
brought me to colour with you, because
I was blue, and summer was not
fulfilling its promises.

Orange, yellow, green
taking shapes and
and shading in.

In the end there was a picture
something we had made
layers and layers of paint
a new perspective.

Watch

Poems for my Grandmother

i. Recovery

I need it too, as I walk with you,
first to the chapel and then to the light box
where your lips move over the words.

It is there in the crook of my arm,
your recovery, the small steps of it,
as we shuffle back to your room
my irises tall in their water bottle.

Outside, after, in a car park lit with sunshine,
I feel the path to love with all its
complications etched in, burned in, sewn in.

I will recover,
and so will you.

ii. Buttons

The buttons are scattered,
no, placed
on a felt square –
hands put them there
chose them, filled a room
with glue fumes.

The grief I've kept at bay
caught up with me today
I became tearful, over buttons,
taken and used by hands
older than yours.

How quick the mind is to
sling images to the front of the brain,
your dextrous fingers typing,
knitting all those scarves and jumpers
and now, one 'alien', photographed for textbooks,
the other, slipping on you, this week.

Our lives are just buttons scattered,
no, placed
we create the pattern
that makes sense to us.

iii. S's and R's

You are struggling with them
the sounds sticking at the back of your tongue
I have no way to help you
only listen and let you go slow.

I am putting love on a plate for you today
I made the pudding your way
I practiced my patience
in this kitchen where you used to mind us.

Later, I cry at the disease
eroding your nerve cells
the name of it suddenly stuck behind my tongue
two 's's', two r's'
too much to take. in.

iv. Clip

The mirror is for you to see yourself
the mirror is for that patch of wall
the builders left unpainted

it goes up with two hooks
and then you struggle with your clip
the hairpin that will keep it all together.

Leaving

The waves crash, they are angry too;
full weight onto the rocks
not a calm tidal pull, it is a rush to renew rage,
a purge, a cleanse, a blackout.

I wish for a clear glass box to step into
and scream, scream and empty
my lungs, show the redness of my throat.
Sometimes the private is our prison,
keeps us in, in the din of mental
merry-go-round, we deafen.

I should have bellowed next to the ocean spray
I should have gotten down on the pavement
and blackened my fists
I should have showed you
my leaving.

What My Brother Said to Me

(After Naomi Shihab Nye)

Seems like you are still running a race,
but the race is *over*.

Pull off your number.
Walk to the barrier.
Go over it and through the crowd.
Don't think about who's watching.

I know you are a great marathon runner
but rest now, it's over.

Balloon

I used to think of you
panicked
like a child who had
let the string slip

and up and up
you went
before I could know
that I had let you go.

Offering

In a church neither of us believes in
I've lit a candle for us both
dashed in from the street after we parted
a heaving in my chest

escaped to a nave to cry in private
tears flowing
I saw hands folding
lotus flowers

sobs carried up like offers
one by one
a salute to us
my love, our love
given somewhere else now.

Whatever I have left I will give freely-
water, salt, blood.

Note to Self

Remember, you are changing
pain to joy
hope to action
rigour to contemplation
fear to goals
sadness to knowledge
will to dreams
love to compassion.

Friends

They are there in their twos
and threes and ones.
They don't pick up the pieces
they see the shattered fragments
clasp their hands to mine
say nothing
soundlessly move me.

Sometimes that's all you need,
a guide to the doorway.

Darkness into Light

We turned night into dawn, sea breeze,
my lungs still too heavy to take it in.

We walked and slow jogged into morning,
grateful for this end to restlessness.

We joined the two thousand yellow lights,
caught our breath, marked a moment.

This Chapter

After this chapter, there will be another,
and another after should I choose
to turn the page,
should I choose
to write the line.

After this chapter, there will
be another opening, should I choose
to welcome it, should I choose
to learn.

After this chapter, I will finish
what I started, begin a different conclusion
draw another card
try another chapter,
choose another 'after'.

Mermaid

It was an enchantment for us both
the long shimmering skin of me
next to your trawler

but now you are gone,
and I must relinquish the water.

I must live on land and learn
to be stronger.
I must turn my back on you and
the horizon

our myth trailing,
coating everything with glitter.

Acknowledgements

The author would like to thank the following people for their help and support:

Thank you Jessie for bringing the book into the world. Thank you Maureen Keith, Finbar McHugh and Siobhán Hutson for working with me on the cover to produce the gold stone!

I am deeply indebted to Elaine Feeney and Elaine Cosgrove. Thank you for your encouragement, your keen eyes and your feedback on this work, it was a privilege and a huge blessing having you both at my side. Thank you mom, dad and Aaron, for your love and support of my writing. Thank you friends for all of your words and kindnesses. A special thank you to the writers who read this manuscript before publication and offered their support.

Some of these poems have previously been published in: *Prelude Magazine* (New York), *Washing the Windows* Anthology (Arlen House, Ireland), and *Freckle* (Northern Ireland).

DANI GILL is a writer, curator, and creative writing tutor, based in the west of Ireland. She has been included in the Irish women's poetry anthology *Washing Windows* (Arlen House, 2016), and publications such as *Prelude* (New York), and *Freckle* (Northern Ireland). From 2010-2016 she was the Director of Cúirt International Festival of Literature, Galway. Dani now works as a freelance curator and creative writing tutor for young people and adults. AFTER LOVE is her first collection.

www.danigill.com   @TheeDaniMagic